MW00761756

Restoring Shattered Lives

By
Dr. Bruno A. Spada

PRESS

Copyright © 2012 by Dr. Bruno A. Spada

Restoring Shattered Lives
by Dr. Bruno A. Spada

Printed in the United States of America

ISBN 9781624197598

All rights reserved solely by the author. The author guarantees all contents are original and do not infringe upon the legal rights of any other person or work. No part of this book may be reproduced in any form without the permission of the author. The views expressed in this book are not necessarily those of the publisher.

Unless otherwise indicated, Bible quotations are taken from the New King James Version, (NKJV). Copyright © 1975 by Thomas Nelson; The New International Version, (NIV). Copyright © 1973 by Biblica, Inc.

www.xulonpress.com

Dr. Bruno A. Spada has been in full-time ministry for more than thirty years. He demonstrates the heart of a pastor and the work of an evangelist. His heart is to see the brokenhearted become whole through the power of Jesus Christ. He and his wife, Robin, have been married nearly thirty years with three children, Simeon, Promise and Serenity.

Special thanks to my beloved wife, Robin, and our children, Simeon, Promise and Serenity, for your love and support. I love all of you very much.

Special thanks to my Father and Mother for always believing in me because of the work of Jesus Christ in my life.

Special thanks to Rev. Terry and Sandy Fairbanks. Thank you for being a mentor.

Special thanks to the Potter's House Church of God for your loving support.

Special thanks to Merle and Mary Jameson who are such blessings to the kingdom of God.

Special thanks to Dottie Woodrum for your energy, joy and kindness. You're a blessing from the Lord.

Special thanks to Bill and Fro Spicer for your continual support and love. May the Lord Jesus grant you grace.

Special thanks to Lino and Kim Aparo. The Lord Jesus bless you for your kindness.

If you would like additional books or study on CD call 860-303-5065

CONTENTS

CHAPTER III. - WINNING THE WAR ON OUR FAMILIES AND RELATIONSHIPS

CHAPTER IV. - NEW LIFE IN CHRIST

INTRODUCTION

RESTORING SHATTERED LIVES

Isaiah 61:1 says, "He hath sent me to bind up the broken-hearted" (KJV). The Hebrew word for brokenhearted is *shaw-bar*, which means to shatter. He has sent me to heal shattered lives. This verse also deals with the inner man. The Hebrew word used is *labe*, which deals with the mind, will, heart and understanding. Healing shattered lives deals with the heart and thinking of a person which affect the appetites, emotions and passions of a person.

The prophet Isaiah tells us, "He hath sent me to bind up the broken-hearted." The brokenhearted are those whose lives have been shattered. Here are four areas to consider concerning broken lives:

1. The war within
2. Inner healing and overcoming the war within
3. Winning the war in our families and relationships
4. New life in Christ

In Isaiah 61:1 the Holy Spirit comes upon a person and causes him to be a healer of broken hearts. In this world filled with people who are brokenhearted due to sorrow, disappointment and/or loss, the Spirit-filled child of God comes with a healing ministry. We are a channel of peace and restoration to the shattered hearts of this world.

CHAPTER I

THE WAR WITHIN

SELAH SELECTION

"But what things were gain to me, these I have counted loss for Christ. Yet indeed I also count all things loss for the excellency of the knowledge of Christ Jesus my Lord, for whom I have suffered the loss of all things, and count them as rubbish, that I may gain Christ" (Philippians 3:7-8, NKJV).

The Greek word for "knowledge" here speaks of a personal, experiential and progressive knowledge. Paul pursued this kind of knowing of Christ. A man cannot make other things his gain and at the same time gain Christ. He who loses all things and even himself on account of Christ gains Christ.

The quest of restoring shattered lives means that we have to engage in spiritual warfare, and the weapon of choice must be the Holy Bible.

BONDAGE AND SPIRITUAL WARFARE

John 10:10 reveals that the enemy of our soul comes to steal, kill and destroy us. One of the ways the enemy of our soul does this is by putting us in bondage through the works of the flesh or the ungodly system of this world. One of the redemptive works of Jesus Christ on the cross of Calvary was to free us from the effects of bondage caused by the lust of the flesh, the lust of the eyes and the pride of life which is in this world, as it says in 1 John 2:16. The Word of God tells us about this warfare found in the world in Hebrews 2:15, Romans 8:15 and Luke 4:18.

In order to minister to shattered lives, the Bible tells us we must address the world, the flesh and the devil, as recorded in Galatians 5:1, John 8:31-36 and Romans 8:2. The Word of God teaches us that true freedom is found in its truths applied to everyday living.

What brought this bondage to the human race? The spiritual war started in the Garden of Eden where two seeds were at work in the universe. Genesis 3:14-15 reveals the seed of Satan, the seed of the woman and the spiritual warfare that exists between the seeds. The results of sin through disobedience brought shame, separation from a relationship with God Almighty, dishonesty, blame and judgment. Jesus Christ's sacrificial death on the cross gives us the opportunity to change our relationship with God through repentance and forgiveness. Jesus Christ came to destroy the work of the devil, according to 1 John 3:8. The devil is described as a murderer and deceiver in John 8:44. One of the works of redemption on the cross of Calvary is having the authority to rule over the kingdom of evil. Knowing Jesus Christ as personal Lord and Savior gives us the assurance that Jesus has won the spiritual war for us on the cross of Calvary as revealed in Matthew 12:22-24.

One of the purposes of the devil is to manipulate you, so you can make bad decisions spiritually, which can lead to spiritual bondage. A spiritual war is going on for your eternal soul. The Bible describes this spiritual war in the book of Daniel, chapter 10. In the New Testament Luke describes how the devil comes to take the Word of God out of the heart and mind of a person by pursuing this world's system and the works of the flesh. The works of the flesh are described in Galatians 5:16 and how the flesh lusts against the Spirit. We are encouraged by the Word of God to be strong in the Lord and in the power of His might. When we put on the whole armor of God we will be able to stand against the wiles of the devil.

We don't wrestle against flesh and blood but against principalities and powers of this world as the Word of God proclaims in Ephesians 6:10-20.

As mentioned, Galatians 5:16 reveals that the flesh lusts against the Spirit; this lust of the flesh can lead to bondage. Bondage affects our thinking, feelings and will. Sin is rooted in the core of the human personality as Romans 5:1-21 tells us.. Bondage or freedom is expressed in our thoughts, behaviors and feelings. The lifestyle of bondage or freedom can be manifested in us physically through our health or through behavioral patterns expressed through addiction and sinful living.

The road to freedom is through the application of the living Word of God. Also, the road to freedom in this spiritual war is acknowledgment of addictions and turning away from its lifestyle, accountability for truth by the Word of God in those who love you and taking responsibility for your actions. Our Father in heaven made provisions for our freedom through the crucifixion of Jesus, so that He can save us from the effects of sin and teach us how to walk in freedom through Jesus Christ. Scriptures that express our freedom are found in Hebrews 2:15, Galatians 5:1, Romans 8:2, Romans 5, 1 John 3:8, Luke 4:18, John 8:31-36, Genesis 3:14-15, Romans 8:15 and Galatians 5:16. The application of the Word of God has the power to give us freedom in our body, thoughts, behaviors and relationships.

A spiritual warfare is going on, according to Ephesians 6:12. The war is against the devil, whom the Bible describes as the tempter in Matthew 4:3, the evil one in 1 John 2:13, the great deceiver in Revelation 12:9, the father of lies and "you shall know the truth and the truth shall make you free" in John 8:32 (KJV). I emphasize the truth *that you know.* Through the sacrifice of Jesus on the cross and the Word of God we can live free from bondage because Jesus Christ has won the spiritual war for us. God is inviting us to spiritual freedom in which strongholds are broken and the life of Christ is lived through us. This life in Christ is a state of intimacy with God, which breaks strongholds, and we can experience spiritual freedom.

Intimacy with God comes through sharing and fellowship with God, which is called communion. The Gospel of John, chapter 17, shows us the intimacy Jesus had with His Father in heaven and how Jesus wanted us to have the same unity with the Father in heaven as Jesus had with Him. Song of Solomon 2:8-10 gives us a picture of how God delights in having a relationship with us. This type of relationship breaks strongholds, gives us new hope and shows us unconditional love. This type of relationship is the power that destroys the work of spiritual warfare that comes from the devil, who is the enemy of our soul, and the work of the flesh. The cross of Jesus Christ displays the greatest act of unconditional love that brought us the spiritual freedom to win the war within.

FORGIVENESS

Another way to win the war within is through the act of forgiveness. Forgiveness removes the buildup of hurt, resentment and anger, which causes us to lose the war within. Without forgiveness love between people and God is damaged. Unforgiveness stops our communion with God and causes us to lose the war within. Unforgiveness can enslave us to our past, and the results will bring pain within.

Forgiveness is the core of Christianity. Even if the other person is not receptive we can still release them. The grace of God was extended to us through Jesus Christ and His sacrifice on the cross. Romans 5:8 tells us, "But God commendeth his love toward us, in that, while we were yet sinners, Christ died for us" (KJV). Forgiveness was extended to us through repentance. We extend forgiveness because it was extended to us through Jesus Christ. Forgiving and releasing others that have hurt us will release us from carrying the act perpetrated against us. Forgiveness is God's heart. To trust may take time; don't confuse the two. The Bible is clear that we are to forgive each other. Unforgiveness can be a reaction to the resentment, bitterness, anger or hostility. Forgiveness is the reaction of releasing others, just as Jesus did for us. He told us in

Mark 11:24-26 that if we have anything against anyone, forgive that person so our Father in heaven will forgive us our trespasses. But if we do not forgive, neither will our Father in heaven forgive our trespasses.

Jesus emphasizes this on several occasions. Luke 6:37 commands us to forgive, and we will be forgiven. In Matthew 6:12 we ask God to forgive our debts as we forgive our debtors. The way we forgive and release is the way we will be forgiven. Scriptures on forgiveness include Psalm 130:4, Mark 3:29, Acts 13:38, Ephesians 1:7 and Colossians 1:14.

The greatest need for mankind is not just economical, political, educational, social, physical or psychological; it's also spiritual. The most fundamental truth of the Bible is that mankind was born into sin and he will never find real joy until he knows the joy of sins forgiven. Mankind needs forgiveness. That's why God sent Jesus Christ to be our Savior. The story of the woman who was forgiven in Luke 7:36-50 shows how she was looked down upon and considered the scum of the town. It was not an easy thing for her to enter that house and present herself to Jesus. She had to get past her own feelings of guilt. Her battle was not just for forgiveness from God; she also had to forgive herself. This shattered life found healing through the compassion and forgiveness of Jesus Christ.

In Luke 15:11-24 we read the story of a younger son who was wild and wasteful. He wanted his father's inheritance so he could go to a far country and waste his substance on riotous living. A famine hit the land, and his money ran out. The Bible says he came back to his senses and turned back toward home, but he had to deal with feelings of unworthiness and guilt. The Bible says that while he was a great way off his father saw him and ran to him, hugged his neck and kissed him. The father tells his servants to go and get his son the best robe, ring, shoes and food. The father represents our heavenly Father. He forgave the son, but this younger son had to forgive himself, which was the spiritual war that was going on in him. This shattered life found forgiveness and healing provided by our heavenly Father through the sacrifice of Jesus Christ on the cross of Calvary.

The results of forgiving oneself are expressed in Romans 8:1, which declares that "there is therefore now no condemnation to them which are in Christ Jesus, who walk not after the flesh, but after the Spirit" (KJV). Psalm 103:12 declares that "as far as the east is from the west, so far hath he removed our transgressions from us" (KJV). First John 1:9 declares, "If we confess our sins, he is faithful and just to forgive us our sins, and to cleanse us from all unrighteousness" (KJV). The power of forgiveness heals shattered lives. David wrote this psalm as an expression of his thankfulness for God's grace in providing the gift of forgiveness: "Blessed is he whose transgressions is forgiven, whose sins is covered" (Psalm 32:1, KJV).

Scriptures on the forgiving power of God can be found in Matthew 9:2, Matthew 9:5, Mark 4:12, Luke 5:20, Luke 6:37, Luke 7:47, Acts 8:22, Romans 4:7, Ephesians 4:32, Colossians 2:13, James 5:15, 1 John 2:12, Psalm 130:4, Ephesians 1:7 and Colossians 1:14. Forgiveness is a matter of God's grace. When you have been forgiven you'll love much. You'll be able, by His grace, to forgive others and yourself. In Luke 23:23-34 (KJV), while Jesus our Savior was being crucified, among His last words were "Father, forgive them; for they do not know what they do." This is the greatest expression of forgiveness from God to the human race.

FINDING SIGNIFICANCE IN LIFE

Another battle concerning winning the war within is dealing with our value and developing a biblical understanding for finding value in this world in which we live. The search for value affects our purpose in life. Feelings of worthlessness and inferiority can be overcome through the love of Jesus Christ. If we don't understand our value as the Bible teaches, we can't help others understand who they are. As human beings we are unique because we are created in the image of God. The very first pages of the Bible talk about this in Genesis 1:27 (KJV), declaring that "So God created man in His own image, in the image of God created he him; male and female created he them."

Everything was created with distinction. The plants sense awareness, animals have self awareness, and humans have God awareness. In Genesis 3 humanity fell because of sin. Sin marred the image of God. The image of God is restored through the redemptive work of Jesus Christ on the cross of Calvary. Our repentance of sin and the forgiveness of God brought us into right standing and a personal relationship with God. The Bible calls this righteousness, which is received through confession, repentance, believing and accepting God's grace.

God knew us before we were born. Psalm 139 shows us this and describes the sovereignty of God. In this chapter the psalmist declares, "My substance was not hid from thee, when I was made in secret, and curiously wrought in the lowest parts of the earth. Thine eyes did see my substance, yet being unperfected; and in thy book all my members were written, which in continuance were fashioned, when as yet there was none of them. How precious also are thy thoughts unto me, O God! How great is the sum of them! If I should count them, they are more in number than the sand; when I awake, I am still with thee" (KJV). We were created by God. It was His idea, and we were shaped for significance.

Distorted view of self can make you believe you have no value. This distortion is caused by a lifestyle dominated by feelings of no value, which lead to a worldview of hopelessness.

This distortion may produce a life that says I have no significance and can be developed by a person's belief system.

If you believe God loves you, as stated in John 3:16, you will find value in this world. We were made in His image and His likeness. Our significance comes from whose we are. As believers in Jesus Christ our value comes from knowing we were created in God's image. Because of this we can have a living relationship with God through Jesus Christ. Jesus came to save us from our sins and restore shattered lives

The answer to this devaluation of life is found in the Bible, the road map for life. God promises us in His Word that with His help all things are possible; that He will strengthen and uphold us; that He loves us and nothing can separate us from His love; and that we can do all things as He strengthens us. God will supply our spiritual need. We can cast all our anxieties on Him, and He will give us His peace that He will never leave us nor forsake us. Jesus said in John 10:10b (KJV), "I have come that they might have life, that they might have it more abundantly." Because of Jesus Christ's promise to us, we have value in this life. Genesis 1:27 declares that we were created in the image of God, and our value is derived from Him.

The Old Testament book of Ecclesiastes teaches us through the life of King Solomon that life is meaningless without God. Ecclesiastes 2:25 reveals that not even eating can be enjoyed without God. He goes on to say in the book of Ecclesiastes that meaning and purpose to life are found in having a relationship with the God of the Bible.

Marital couples suffer in the area of significance because they long to be heard, affirmed and praised, to feel safe, to be touched and to be desired passionately. When these areas are not fulfilled we will look for substitutes in order to be fulfilled and significant. People hurt spiritually, emotionally, relationally; many times this brings hurt, pain and anger to our lives. The housewife who is wounded in her spirit because she doesn't feel close to her husband, whose father was an alcoholic and mother was very demanding, will not feel lovable. She does not believe she has value, and because of this she can't receive her husband's love. These emotions can be healed and restored through the Lord Jesus Christ, as we face these emotions and present them to the Lord. The husband who never received affirmation from his father, can cause him to be demanding and unforgiving to his wife.

The psalmist David wrote about presenting his emotions and life to God. In Psalm 51:6 we read, "Surely you desire truth in the inner parts; you teach me wisdom in the inmost place" (NIV). David expressed himself to the Lord as he often did, confronting his emotions so the Lord could heal and lead him through life. David wrote about his despair and difficult situations. In Psalm

55:4-5 he cried out, "My heart is in anguish within me; the terrors of death assail me. Fear and trembling have beset me; horror has overwhelmed me" (NIV). David also communicated his despair to the Lord in Psalm 44:24-25: "Why do you hide your face and forget our misery and oppression? We are brought down to the dust; our bodies cling to the ground" (NIV). David found out the greatest way to deal with his emotions was to present them to God. The God of the Bible will produce the significance we are looking for in life if we believe and follow Him. False belief says I must meet certain standards to feel good about myself. God's truth says I am deeply loved by God, which is ultimately expressed by Jesus Christ's death on the cross. First John 4:10 reveals, "Herein is love, not that we loved God, but that he loved us, and sent his son to be the propitiation for our sins" (KJV). This is stating that Jesus is our atoning sacrifice for our sins. False belief says I must have the approval of others to feel good about myself. God's truth says because of justification I am completely forgiven by and fully pleasing to God. I no longer have to fear failure. Romans 5:18 declares, "Therefore as by the offense of one judgment came upon all men to condemnation; even so by the righteousness of one the free gift came upon all men unto justification of life" (KJV).

False belief says that those who fail are unworthy of love and deserve to be punished. God's truth says that those turning from sin and confessing Jesus as Savior have become new creatures. All things are new in me because of what Jesus did for me on the cross. I no longer need to experience the pain of shame. In Titus 3:5 we read, "Not by works of righteousness which we have done, but according to his mercy he has saved us, by the washing of regeneration, and renewing of the Holy Ghost" (KJV). False belief says I am what I am, I cannot change, and I am hopeless. God's truth says because of what Jesus did for me on the cross, I am totally accepted by God. I no longer have to fear rejection. Hebrews 2:17 states, "Wherefore in all things it behooved him to be like unto his brethren, that he might be a merciful and faithful high priest in things pertaining to God, to make reconciliation for the sins of the people" (KJV).

Many in life don't feel significant because they may have come from a dysfunctional family. They say things like, "Nobody will ever love me; if people really knew who I was they wouldn't like me; I've been a failure all my life, and I guess I'll always be a failure; I'll never be able to change; not even God really cares about me." When we realize the God of the Bible is a God of love and that He's passionate about us, the significance we look for in life will be present because of God's love. The experience of God's love and provision allows us to trust God and is developed through applying the Word of God. The love of God is greater than the love of our parents. Psalm 103:13 declares, "As a father has compassion on his children, so the Lord has compassion on those who fear him" (NIV). Isaiah 49:15 asks, "Can a mother forget the baby at her breast and have no compassion on the child she has borne? Though she may forget, I will not forget you" (NIV). Understanding that God loves us and has purpose for our lives makes us creatures of value. Colossians 3:23-24 tells us God has called us to work for Him: "Whatever you do, do it heartily, as to the Lord and not to men, knowing that from the Lord you will receive the reward of the inheritance; for you serve the Lord Christ" (NKJV).

The entire Bible gives witness to the truth that God, from eternity, chose to work through His people to accomplish His eternal purpose in this world. When God was about to destroy this earth because of sin He called Noah and his family, who were saved from destruction. This is found in the book of Genesis, chapters 6–10. When God wanted to establish saving faith (salvation) for all mankind He chose Abraham (Genesis 12:22; Hebrews 11:8). When God was ready to deliver the children of Israel from bondage to Egypt He called Moses to Himself and sent him to be the one through whom He would accomplish this task. This is recorded in Exodus 3. The fact that God has chosen to use people to accomplish His purpose can be seen throughout the Bible. Fulfilling a purpose greater than ourselves, through our talents and skills, can bring great significance to our lives.

God wants to work through me and you to accomplish His work on this earth. Jesus Christ fulfilled redemption for all sinners on the cross of Calvary. Our faith and trust in Him as our Savior is the beginning of our significance in this world. We are all creatures of destiny; destiny is the result of the choices and decisions we make every day.

We have opportunities before us every day to increase our knowledge and wisdom through the Word of God and life's circumstances. The wisest man that ever lived next to Jesus Christ said this in Ecclesiastes 9:11: "I returned, and saw under the sun, that the race is not to the swift, nor the battle to the strong, nor bread to the wise, nor yet riches to men of understanding, nor yet favor to men of skill; but times and chance happen to them all" (NKJV).

One of the greatest stories of finding value and fulfilling one's purpose is that of Abraham Lincoln. It is a great example of a man struggling to release the wealth of potential that was inside him and thus fulfilling the significance of his life. Looking at the struggles of his life it is amazing that he became one of the greatest presidents America has ever known. Let's look at some of the struggles he faced. He lost his job; he was elected to the legislature; he suffered the death of his sweetheart; he suffered a nervous breakdown; he was defeated for speaker of the state legislature; he was defeated for nomination for Congress; he was elected to Congress; he was rejected for the position of land officer; he was defeated for the Senate; he was defeated for the nomination for vice president of the United States. President Lincoln fulfilled his destiny and lived a life of value.

We can fulfill God's plan for us. Colossians 1:16 declares, "For by him all things were created, that are in heaven, and that are in earth, visible and invisible, whether they be thrones, or dominions, or principalities, or powers: all things were created by him, and for him" (KJV). We can look to the Holy Bible for salvation, direction, guidance and the fulfillment of purpose in this life. We are people of value according to the God of the Bible.

This journey to destiny starts with accepting Christ as Lord and Savior.

FREEDOM THROUGH JESUS CHRIST THAT CAN HELP OTHERS

Jesus Christ brings freedom through which bondages are broken and our habits become ways of life that lead to freedom spiritually. What does the Word of God say about this subject? In Psalm 16:9 we read, "Therefore my heart is glad, and my glory rejoiceth: my flesh also will rest in hope" (KJV). Matthew 4:16 says, "The people who sat in darkness have seen a great light, and upon those who sat in the region and shadow of death light has dawned. From that time Jesus began to preach and say, 'Repent, for the kingdom of heaven is at hand'" (KJV). In Matthew 6:31-33 we see, "So do not worry, saying, 'What shall we eat?' or 'What shall we drink?' or 'What shall we wear?' For the pagans run after all these things, and your heavenly Father knows that you need them. But seek first his kingdom and his righteousness, and all these things will be given to you as well" (NIV).

Genesis 2:8-9 states, "And the Lord God planted a garden eastward in Eden; and there he put the man whom he had formed and out of the ground made the Lord God to grow every tree that is pleasant to the sight, and good for food; the tree of life also in the midst of the garden, and the tree of the knowledge of good and evil" (KJV). Genesis 2:15-17 declares, "And the Lord God took the man, and put him into the Garden of Eden to dress it and to keep it. And the Lord God commanded the man, saying, of every tree of the garden thou mayest freely eat: but of the tree of the knowledge of good and evil, you shall not eat of it: for in the day that thou eatest thereof thou shalt surely die." (KJV).

In Genesis 3:4-10 we read, "And the serpent said unto the woman, ye shall not surely die: For God doth know that in the day ye eat thereof, then your eyes shall be opened, and ye shall be as gods, knowing good and evil. And when the woman saw that the tree was good for food, and that it was pleasant to the eyes, and a tree to be desired to make one wise, she took of the fruit thereof, and did eat, and gave also unto her husband with her; and he did eat. And the eyes of them both were opened, and they knew that they were naked; and they sewed fig leaves together, and made themselves aprons. And they heard the voice of the Lord God walking in the garden in the cool of the day: and Adam and his wife hid themselves from the presence of the Lord God amongst the trees of the garden. Then the Lord God called to Adam, and said unto him, Where art thou? And he said, I heard thy voice in the garden, and I was afraid, because I was naked; and I hid myself" (KJV).

The apostle Paul reminds us in 2 Timothy 1:7, "For God has not given us a spirit of fear, but of power, and of love, and of a sound mind" (KJV). Spiritual freedom is found in drawing closer to God our Father. One of the miracles of Jesus Christ is that He has shown us how to know our Father in heaven as Abba Daddy. John 17:3 reveals, "And this is life eternal, that they might know thee the only true God, and Jesus Christ, whom thou hast sent" (KJV). When we love the God of the Bible we will trust, obey and glorify Him because of the sacrifice of His Son Jesus Christ on the cross of Calvary.

Spiritual freedom is discovered in Jesus Christ, which means a living relationship with Him through the Bible. . Spiritual freedom comes through Jesus Christ and a loving relationship with God our heavenly Father through the sacrificial death of Jesus Christ. This relationship is expressed through fellowship with God our Father that Jesus made possible on the cross of Calvary. Through repentance and faith in Jesus Christ we can speak to God the Father anytime. Our relationship can lead to communion; Jesus Christ gives us the desire to experience union, a living relationship with God as our Father in heaven. This living relationship is expressed through prayer, the place where you are free from distractions. The position is where you're free to talk to your heavenly Father. This is the place where everything slows down, and the activities of the day are not important at that moment. The purpose is to commune with God our

Father in the name of Jesus Christ and for Him to commune with us through the Bible by His holy Spirit. When this becomes part of our lives, the presence of God is with us.

One of the hindrances to spiritual freedom is idols. The God of the Bible is the only one who can satisfy us. The Word of God tells us in Philippians 4:19, "But my God shall supply all your need according to His riches in glory by Christ Jesus" (KJV).

Value can't come by looking to others to see what they think of us. The Word of God tells us Jesus gave Himself for us and that He loves us. Galatians 2:20 says, "I am crucified with Christ; nevertheless I live; yet not I, but Christ liveth in me: and the life which I now live in the flesh I live by faith of the Son of God, who loved me, and gave himself for me." (KJV). Hebrews 13:5 states "Let your conduct be without covetousness; be content with such things as you have. For he himself has said, 'I will never leave you nor forsake you'" (NKJV).

Another hindrance to spiritual freedom is disaffection toward God or losing hope. In 2 Corinthians 11:2-3 we read that God is jealous for us: "For I am jealous for you with godly jealousy. For I have betrothed you to one husband, that I may present you as a chaste virgin to Christ" (NKJV). What takes us from a place of trusting God and rendering our affection to Him to losing heart in God? The stress and strain of life can cause this. James 1:2-4 tells us to "count it all joy when you fall into various trials, knowing the testing of your faith produces patience. But let patience have its perfect work, that you may be perfect and complete, lacking nothing" (KJV). The word "perfect" here in the Greek is *tel-i-os*, which when translated means *mature*. Trials are designed to develop and mature Christians in this world. We have the same choices in life of receiving or refusing what Jesus Christ has provided for us. We were born into different families with different problems, but the Lord Jesus Christ can bring healing.. John 8:32 states, "And you shall know the truth, and the truth shall make you free" (NKJV). This spiritual freedom can help others change.

In a world of technology there is a depletion of faith in God and the truth about His Word. The problems of this world can ultimately be traced back to the fall of Adam and Eve. This relationship with Jesus can bring change to others. We must go back to the beginning to the first man and woman. God created them to be physically and spiritually alive and intimately related to Him. But when Eve was deceived and Adam sinned they died spiritually and were separated from God. Physical death was also a consequence; God's perfect creation was thrown into chaos.

Fear was the first emotion recorded in Scripture after the fall. Adam said, "I was afraid because I was naked; and I hid myself" (Genesis 3:10, NKJV). Anxiety disorders can lead to a disconnection from the living God. The born-again experience is only the beginning of a life of trust in Jesus Christ, who by faith saved us from our sins as we repented and turned to Him.

The other very important part of wholeness is found in Romans 12:2: "And do not be conformed to this world, but be transformed by the renewing of your mind, that you may prove what is that good and acceptable and perfect will of God" (NKJV). Others can change as they develop a relationship with the God of the Bible.

Coaching is motivating and inspiring others to grow. Coaching is proactive and causes them to look ahead. Coaching helps others build vision and look to the future. Another way to help others change is teaching them to become disciples. Jesus told Peter in Matthew 4:19, "Follow Me, and I will make you fishers of men" (NKJV). In Acts 1:8b Jesus said, "Ye shall be witnesses unto me both in Jerusalem, and in all Judea, and in Samaria, and unto the uttermost part of the earth" (KJV).

The first thing we must have others do is answer the call to discipleship. In Matthew 28:18-20 we read, "And Jesus came and spoke to them, saying, 'All authority has been given to me in heaven and earth. Go therefore and make disciples of all the nations, baptizing them in the name of the Father and of the Son and of the Holy Spirit, teaching them to observe all things I have commanded you; and lo, I am with you always, even to the end of the age. Amen" (NKJV).

To become a disciple-maker involves a deeper commitment to the teaching and principles of Jesus Christ. Examples of this are humbly serving others (John 13:3-15, KJV); counting the cost as warned in

Luke 14:34-35 (KJV); remaining in Christ which will cause you to bear much fruit (John 15:5-8, KJV); calling others to follow Jesus (John 1:35-45, KJV).

One of the simplest meanings of a disciple is a "learner or follower of Christ." One of the keys to helping others change after they have repented is to help them to forget those things which are behind and to press toward the mark of the high calling in Christ Jesus, as declared in Philippians 3:13-14 (KJV). We can help others change by becoming a mentor. A mentor has the ability to see positive change in the mentored. Everyone in need of change needs a father figure to love them and guide them. God's will for our lives, through the sacrifice of Jesus Christ on the cross of Calvary, is the principle of Romans 8:29. It reveals how God predestined us to be conformed to the image of Jesus Christ through mentors, coaches, and leadership. We are helpers of one another, Proverbs 27:17 declares, "As iron sharpens iron, so a man sharpens the countenance of his friend" (NKJV).

POEM PAUSE

REMEMBERING CALVARY
Remembering Calvary
Through the eyes of a mother,
Soldiers leading her Son
To the slaughter.
Her perfect lamb pure and white as snow;
Her precious child, Savior of the world.

Remembering Calvary
Through the eyes of a soldier,
Who does he think he is?
Wanting me to believe!
Yet something I feel I see;
Compassion looked at me.
Could I dare believe
A King would die to set me free?

Remembering Calvary
Through the eyes of a thief,
Hanging there beside this man from Galilee.
He is so full of Love.
It *must* be from above.
Please forgive and remember me
When You enter paradise.

Remembering Calvary
He set the captives free.
The holy Son of God
Made true our victory.
He lived and died to give
This world a hope to live,
Our precious Lord,
The Savior of the world.

By R. J. Thompson

CHAPTER 2

WHOLENESS AND OVERCOMING THE WAR WITHIN

SELAH SELECTION

"Who shall separate us from the love of Christ? Shall tribulation, or distress, or persecution, or famine, or nakedness, or peril, or sword?

Yet in all these things we are more than conquerors through Him who loved us" (Romans 8:35, NKJV). Trials do not separate us from Christ's love; rather, "through him that loved us" we are victorious over them. Nothing can divide us from the love of God in Christ Jesus.

OVERCOMING DEPRESSION AND ITS EFFECTS

Scriptures that talk about depression are found in Psalm 40:1-3, "I waited patiently for the Lord; and he inclined to me, and heard my cry. He also brought me up out of a horrible pit, out of the miry clay, and set my feet upon a rock, and established my steps. He has put a new song in my mouth- Praise to our God; many will see it and fear, and will trust in the LORD." (NKJV); Psalm 147:3, "He heals the brokenhearted and binds up their wounds" (NKJV); Isaiah 41:10, "Fear not, for I am with you; be not dismayed, for I am your God. I will strengthen you, yes, I will help you, I will uphold you with my righteous right hand" (NKJV).

Romans 8:28 declares, "And we know that all things work to the good to those who love God, to those who are called according to His purpose" (NKJV). Depression and mood disorders are major health problems today. Clinical depression is a major depressive disorder, and it's not just a sign of personal weakness or spiritual problems. Depression is the number one cause of disability in the United States. It causes more sick days in our society than diabetes or heart attacks. Some of the symptoms of depression are feelings of sadness, loss of interest and pleasure in hobbies, change in appetite, change in sleep, anxiety and irritability, feelings of hopelessness and helplessness, and crying spells.

The Bible gives insight to healing, spiritual guidance and a balanced lifestyle that can help us overcome depression. Managing your lifestyle is very important concerning depression. You need to get enough exercise, if you're physically able, and also enough sleep with a proper diet.

The first five books of the Bible reveal the emotions, desires and suffering of the people of God. In Psalm 43 the psalmist is unhappy and in trouble. That is why he cries out with these words, "Why art thou cast down, O my soul?" (KJV) In the psalms David was found many times crying out to God in his trouble. This caused him to be dependent on God no matter what emotion he was dealing with at the time. In the Bible Job, Moses, Jonah, Peter and the whole nation of Israel experienced depression. Jeremiah the prophet wrote a whole book of lamentations. Elijah saw God's mighty power at work on Mount Carmel, but when Jezebel threatened to murder Elijah, he fled into the wilderness where he plunged into despondency.. He wanted to die, but God sent an angel to deliver him.

Revenge sometimes leads to destructive violent actions, and violence is not the lifestyle of a Christian. Many people try to hide their feelings but need instead to find a way of positively venting their feelings. Depression may be a form of repressed anger, and that is why positive venting is important. Emotional disappointments can lead to depression. Disappointment, losses, rejection and failures come to everyone, and these lead to periods of unhappiness and discouragement. Learning to accept what you can't change can minimize depression. We learn to trust God as the apostle Paul. Paul's writings from prison stated he had learned to be content in whatever state he was in. Paul learned how to live joyfully, both in poverty and in prosperity. He learned how to trust God, and this helped prevent depression.

Expect discouragement. Jesus warned that we would have problems. The apostle James wrote that trials and temptations would come to test our faith and teach us patience. Consider Jesus Christ at the time of His crucifixion. He was deeply distressed and openly acknowledged His agony. Jesus trusted His Father, but He expected pain and was not surprised when it came. When we are realistic enough to expect pain and informed enough to know God is always in control, then we can handle discouragement better and often keep from slipping into deep depression.

Learn to manage anger and guilt. Some people slide into depression because their minds dwell on past injustices or past failures. Forgiveness becomes critical—forgiving others and yourself. When you dwell on past events and linger in thoughts of anger, guilt and the misery of discouragement, this may cause you to avoid releasing others and yourself through forgiveness. If individuals can learn to handle anger and guilt, much depression can be prevented.

Philippians 4:8 teaches us about the power of meditation in the Word of God. The Bible teaches us things that are good, positive and just. Meditation on God's Word directs our minds away from thinking what is negative. Finding support in the Bible and with people who love us unconditionally can do much to soften the trauma of crises and provide strength and help in times of need. When you realize you're not alone, you're able to cope better and avoid severe depression. Poor diet and lack of exercise, when physically able, can make people depression prone. Some causes of depression are the death of a loved one, loss of a friendship, loss of a job or lifestyle transition, loss of self-esteem, stress issues and pressures at home or at work. Depression is a common struggle and treatable through various ways God has made available. Faulty ways of thinking can be defeated through the power of the Bible and its application.

Our dependence on the God of the Bible will combat depression. Jesus reveals that God blesses those who realize their need for Him in Matthew 5:3 (KJV). God's resources cannot be earned; they can only be received as a gift when we, in humility, acknowledge our need for our Creator. He can provide what we need to overcome the most severe depression.

Psalm 142 is a picture of the cycle of discouragement and loneliness that can lead to depression. David gives a detailed description of his loneliness. He says he is in despair; his spirit is stifled within him. He has been deserted, and his feelings of disorientation and desertion have resulted in depression. He is defeated and has no hope for the future. David teaches us to verbalize our emotions to God; he paints God a picture of how he feels. David realized God's provision, and when he sees His strength his problem begins to fade away.

Jesus gives us a way out as believers in dealing with depression. In Matthew 11:28-30 He said, "Come unto me, all you who labor and are heavy laden, and I will give you rest. Take my yoke upon you and learn from me, for I am gentle and lowly in heart, and you will find rest for your souls. For my yoke is easy and my burden is light" (NKJV).

Elijah is a great example of how depression can strike even the boldest and most godly men. He became so stricken he retreated to a cave and wanted to die (1 Kings 19:4). God provided him with food, sent angels to minister to his loneliness and brought him to a place of rest. Elijah received God's loving care and was eventually restored in strength and purpose. God is no respecter of persons and will minister to all who will call to Him in the name of Jesus Christ, the one who died on the cross of Calvary to set us free from the effects of sin. God will minister the very same way today to anyone who suffers in the dark places of depression. Philippians 4:6-7 tells us to be anxious for nothing, but "by prayer and supplication, with thanksgiving, let your request be know to God" (KJV). God wants to change the distorted thinking of the depressed to the accurate, realistic and wholesome thinking of the Word of God.

STRESS AND ANXIETY: OVERCOMING FEAR, PHOBIAS AND PANIC DISORDERS

Anxiety is pervasive and widespread. It affects people of all ages. The holy Scriptures, written by holy men who wrote the Bible as the Holy Spirit inspired them to write, as declared in 2 Timothy 3:16, have a lot to say about stress and anxiety. As noted above, Philippians 4:6-7 tells us to have "anxiety for nothing, but in everything by prayer and supplication, with thanksgiving, let your request be make known to God" (KJV). Proverbs 12:25 reveals that "anxiety in the heart of man causes depression, but a good word makes it glad" (KJV). Isaiah 50:4a affirms, "The Lord God has given me the tongue of the learned, that I should know how to speak a word in season to him who is weary" (NKJV).

Anxiety results from a combination of chemical reactions in the brain to stimulus; fearful and worrisome thinking, as well as troubled feelings, only feed anxiety. Anxiety, in effect, can be a stressor or can be caused by stress. Anxiety, like stress, is an inevitable part of life. Symptoms and intensity range from a mild response to a stressful or challenging situation to intense fear and troublesome disorder, which interferes with daily functioning and a sense of well-being. Anxiety can result from a number of other factors such as a painful childhood, major stress or trauma, medical illness, alcohol or drug abuse, and can also occur for no obvious or apparent reason. Stress and our response to it, a sense of helplessness, the duration of the stress and the lack of recovery from the stressor bombarding us can cause damage emotionally and physically. When any stress is prolonged (good or bad), chronic, excessive and intense; when we are not able to recover or remove ourselves from it, there is a transition into distress (stress disease). This causes adrenaline exhaustion and begins to erode the foundation of mental and physical health. The mind and body are not equipped to handle the process of ongoing chronic stress.

The National Institute of Mental Health (NIMH) ranks anxiety disorders as the most common mental health problem in the United States. The NIMH has found more than nineteen million adults suffer from anxiety-related problems. An anxiety-related problem includes panic attacks, which are an intense state of fear that occurs for no apparent reason and is characterized by four or more of the following symptoms:

1. Shortness of breath (dyspnea) or smothering sensations.
2. Dizziness, unsteady feelings or faintness.
3. Palpitations or accelerated heart rate (tachycardia).
4. Trembling or shaking.
5. Numbness or tingling sensation (paresthesias), usually in the fingers, toes or lips.
6. Flushes (hot flashes) or chills.
7. Chest pain or discomfort.
8. Fear of becoming seriously ill or dying.
9. Fear of going crazy or doing something uncontrolled.
10. Sweating.
11. Choking.
12. Nausea or abdominal distress.
13. Feelings of unreality (depersonalization or derealization).

An attack with fewer than four of the above symptoms is called a limited symptom attack. Categories of serious stress disorders can be divided into two main categories. The first is acute stress, which is a reaction to an immediate threat, danger or loss eliciting the fight or flight response. Acute stress meets the diagnostic criteria if it lasts less than six months. It is sudden in onset then usually diminishes once the threat is over. The second is chronic stress, involving a constant ongoing stressful situation, even a seemingly minor one, that is not short-lived and can cause continual pressure that then becomes chronic. This is a more serious form of stress disorder, even though it may not seem as intense as acute stress. Ongoing highly pressured work, long-term relationship problems, loneliness, complicated bereavement, persistent financial worries—all can meet the criteria if this disturbance continues. Eventually this form of stress can weaken the immune system and cause many damaging effects to health and well-being.

Teens are growing up in a different world, trying to meet the challenge of a changing world. These stress problems can lead to greater problems, such as depression and related issues, than the previous generation encountered. The good news is that great advancements have been made in helping people understand and treat this problem. Panic anxiety is also affecting the world today. One of the reasons for stress is because of the hurried hassled lives we now live. The pace of modern life is stretching us out of our limits. A life that won't slow down will eventually shut down. If there is a word that describes the condition of the world today it's overload. People today are overwhelmed, overworked, overcommitted, overanxious, overmatched and overextended. Many are overwhelmed by the pace, pressure and pain of life. The pace of life is expressed in the term 24/7. The Bible promises us peace that comes from God the Father through Jesus Christ. Many have been deceived. Lie number one says, "You can have it all." You really can't have it all, and even if you could where would you put it all? In the Bible the book of Ecclesiastes was written by a king by the name of Solomon who literally had it all. Solomon said, "I did not withhold my heart from any pleasure, for my heart rejoiced in all my labor; and this was my reward for all my labor. Therefore I hated my life because the work that was done under the sun was distressing to me,for all is vanity and grasping for the wind. (Ecclesiastes 2:10, 17-20, NKJV).

Lie number two declares, "You can do it all." We know we can't do it all. If we look at our daily schedules, and an outsider observes our daily schedules, chances are they may think otherwise. Solomon shows us that having it all and doing it all only leads to futility. People with anxiety-related problems often feel as if they're alone. Anxiety-related problems often occur with other issues such as depression, eating disorders and substance abuse. The word "stress" was originally an engineering term used to refer to the amount of force a beam or other physical object could bear without collapsing under the strain. Everyone is under stress. Stress is a normal part of life. As long as we keep that stress within reasonable limits, such as getting rest from it all, we can have a healthy balance. Mental stress can come from worrying, which is continually thinking about something without a solution.

Delighting ourselves in the Lord will reduce stress, as instructed in Psalm 37:4-5: "Delight yourself also in the Lord, and he shall give you the desires of your heart. Commit your way to the LORD, Trust also in Him, and He shall bring it to pass" (NKJV). The peace of God, which is provided through Jesus Christ and what He did for us on the cross of Calvary, is ours by faith in Jesus Christ. "And the peace of God, which surpasses all understanding, will guard your hearts and minds through Christ Jesus" (Philippians 4:7, NKJV). Being reminded of what Jesus has done for us brings rest for our souls. "But you are a chosen people, a royal priesthood, a holy nation, a people belonging to God, that you may declare the praises of him who called you out of darkness into his wonderful light. Once you were not a people, but now you are the people of God; once you have not received mercy, but now you have received mercy" (1 Peter 2:9-10, NIV).

The United States spends billions of dollars a year on alcoholism and other addictions. Many thousands of people die each year because of alcoholism, and many child abuse cases are related to alcohol. The Bible has many things to say about alcohol. Solomon warns about alcoholism in Proverbs 23:29-35: "Who has woe? Who has sorrow? Who has contentions? Who has complaints? Who has wounds without cause? Who has redness of eyes? Those who linger long at the wine, those who go in search of mixed wine. Do not look on the wine when it is red, when it sparkles in the cup, when it swirls around smoothly; at last it bites like a serpent, and stings like a viper. Your eyes will see strange things, and your heart will utter perverse things. Yes, you will be like one who lies down in the midst of the sea, or like one who lies at the top at a mast, saying: 'they have struck me, but I was not hurt; they have beaten me, but I did not feel it. When shall I awake, that I may seek another drink?'" (KJV).

The consequences are obvious in the book of Proverbs: hallucinations, saying crazy things, staggering under its influence. Spiritually speaking it's sinful to give control of your body to a substance. One can have a possible genetic disposition, and this may be a factor where there is a family history of it. Socially, college students have drunk themselves to death. Many homes and individuals have been destroyed from the effects of alcohol. We must understand that addiction is a family issue.

How can you tell when someone has a problem? They feel the need to cut down others, they feel guilty, and they feel the need for a morning eye opener so they go to the bottle. You can refer the person to a speakers' meeting; sometimes hospitals offer them to the public for free.

Here is a list of highly addictive drugs: heroin, methadone and codeine. Stimulants that increase your activity are cocaine, amphetamines and crack. Hallucinogenic LSD, mescaline, PCP and angel dust cause hallucination. Pot is the gateway drug that can lead to many other drugs; the effects are similar to alcohol. Other addictions, such as sexual addiction, are permeating all of society. Online sex has crept into our society as well. Gambling is also highly addictive and is growing in the United States.

Spiritually the Bible has the ability to transform our minds. "I beseech you therefore, brethren, by the mercies of God, that you present your bodies a living sacrifice, holy, acceptable to God, which is your reasonable service. And do not be conformed to this world, but be transformed by the renewing of your mind, that you may prove what is that good and acceptable and perfect will of God" (Romans 12:1-2, NKJV). The Word of God gives us hope and wholeness. God wants us to be whole. Emotional health is about having peace about who you are, what you're doing and where you're going. When you know God's purpose in your life and are following Jesus Christ, He can help you manage your mind and emotions to be freed from stress. These elements implemented in your life can help you live a life of wholeness:

1. Release the past and walk in forgiveness. Remember that Jesus Christ died on the cross for your sins and mine.
2. Obey and follow the Word of God. God's book to us of wholeness is the road map to life.
3. Remove yourself from anything that can harm you. God has a plan and a purpose for you.
4. Know that if God is for you nothing can be against you.

The addict represents someone who has become trapped in a web of deceit and dark forces too powerful to overcome without significant help from God and others. In Romans 7:21-25 Paul tells us about the pattern of addictive habits: "I find then a law, that evil is present with me, the one who wills to do good. For I delight in the law of God according to the inward man. But I see another law in my members, warring against the law of my mind, and bringing me into captivity to the law of sin which is in my members. Oh wretched man that I am! Who will deliver me from this body of death? I thank God –through Jesus Christ our Lord! So then, with the mind I myself serve the law of God, but with the flesh the law of sin." (NKJV).

In these Scripture verses Paul shows us the journey of those who struggle with addiction. Addicts know they need to stop using certain substances or doing certain behaviors but seemingly can't. Addicts know they must start doing positive behaviors but will not. Paul also describes the shameful nature of an addict: "Oh wretched man that I am!" The feeling of being bad and worthless is common to all addicts. Addictive behavior perpetuates guilt. Addicts feel helpless and unworthy. Addicts cycle through feelings of the high of addiction and the despair of worthlessness. They may stubbornly resist giving up the high because they feel it's the only solution to the despair.

Many addicts feel lonely and abandoned. They long for love, affirmation and nurture. In many cases the substance or behavior is a substitute for true love and fellowship. This may take many forms. Alcoholics may find a friend in the bottle or being around other drinkers. Food addicts may have certain comfort foods they binge on. Feelings of loneliness and abandonment lead to feelings of anger and resentment. Addicts have developed strong, highly programmed, even automatic behavior patterns in order to maintain their addiction. They will go to extraordinary lengths to deny, minimize or rationalize this addictive behavior. All addicts will need to change certain behavior patterns that lead them into their use. Alcoholics need to select their friends carefully. Food addicts may need to be careful about viewing foods until they can get control and have meals at regular times religiously.

Nehemiah 4 offers a great battle cry to the people. He tells them to fight for their brothers, sons and daughters, wives and their homes. Nehemiah knew the attack from the enemy could come at any time and at the weakest place. He resolved to change their thinking and behavior in times of weakness and attack.

Any addict should have daily phone calls from a person who can keep them accountable. Here are some things to understand about being accountable:

1. I can never do this alone.
2. Fellowship with those who are free from addiction.
3. Understand times of weakness will come.

When the Jewish people wanted to return to Egypt and live as slaves rather than go to the Promised Land, it was Joshua who reminded them to depend on God. Leaders like Joshua can also be found in those recovering people who have achieved a number of years of sobriety. These recovering people who can encourage you have trusted the God of the Bible and understand it can heal and deliver you from addiction in your life and trust Jesus Christ who died on the cross to set us free from any bondage.

LIBERTY THROUGH CHRIST HOPE FOR

THE ADDICT, THE BROKENHEARTED AND
THE EVIL-MINDED

The creation account states that humanity is made in the image of God and consists of natural and spiritual elements. The Bible is the only authoritative explanation of the origin and nature of the soul, and it's imperative we understand how the body, soul and spirit function together in a relationship with God the Father through Jesus Christ, which brings liberty to our lives. There is hope for all because of the transforming ability of the Word of God through Jesus Christ. The old man spiritually and his bondages have been liberated through Jesus Christ; this is where we get the term "new man."

The creation account in the book of Genesis tells us Adam was created in God's image. He was alive physically and spiritually — soul/spirit in union with the body. After the fall of man through sin, insecurity was immediately evident. New believers in Christ will find that strongholds and flesh patterns must be broken. The first emotion Adam expressed in the garden after the fall was fear. The gospel provides redemption for the spiritual death that took place in the garden. Romans 12:2 tells us what takes place after we put our faith in Jesus Christ as Lord and Savior (KJV). It tells us not to be conformed to this age but to be transformed by the renewing of our minds that we may discern what is the will of God, what is good, pleasing and perfect. We are given a new identity through faith in Jesus Christ. Second Corinthians 5:17 declares, "Therefore, if anyone is in Christ, he is a new creation; old things have passed away; behold, all things have become new" (NKJV). Before coming to know Jesus Christ as Lord and Savior, we had a worldview, strongholds and flesh patterns. But through Jesus Christ we have been given liberty and hope in our spirit, soul and body.

Understanding that Jesus is the King of kings, then dethroning ourselves and making Him the only King in our lives will prevent pride from destroying us, so that we can live a life of liberty through Christ and not allow any addiction to control us. God wants us to experience abundant life in Jesus Christ by knowing and believing in Him, by glorifying Him, finding satisfaction in Him, experiencing His peace, enjoying His presence.

Knowing God as Abba Father brings spiritual liberty to our lives and keeps us from a life of addiction. Jesus is our example of this kind of relationship as shown in John 17:1&3: "Jesus spoke these words, lifted up his eyes to heaven, and said: 'Father, the hour has come. Glorify your Son, that your Son also may glorify you,' And this is eternal life, that they may know you, the only true God, and Jesus Christ whom you have sent" (NKJV). Romans 8:15 says, "For you did not receive the spirit of bondage again to fear, but you received the spirit of adoption by whom we cry out, 'Abba, Father'" (NKJV).

God repeatedly calls His children to make space in their lives to know Him. "Be still, and know that I am God; I will be exalted among the nations, I will be exalted in the earth!" (Psalm 46:10, NKJV). An intimate relationship is one in which both persons are fully known and fully loved, with no fear of rejection. This genuine intimacy requires trust, and it takes time to know people well enough to trust them. Develop an environment of communication with God through silence and solitude, Scripture reading and meditation, and then ask Him to reveal Himself through the Word. Prayer is two-way communication. God speaks His thoughts to my thoughts through the Holy Bible by His Spirit. This relationship with God surpasses mere intellectual comprehension. "That Christ may dwell in your hearts through faith; that you, being rooted and grounded in love, may be able to comprehend with all the saints what is the width and length and depth and height- to know the love of Christ which passes knowledge; that you may be filled with all the fullness of God" (Ephesians 3:17-19, NKJV).

When we are free from fear, we willingly want to obey God because of this love relationship we have with God our Father through Jesus Christ. There are barriers to living life in Abba's arms. Our old life without Jesus Christ can be a barrier. "Stand fast therefore in the liberty by which Christ has made us free, and do not be entangled again with a yoke of bondage" (Galatians 5:1, NKJV). Becoming too busy can be a barrier. Pursuing God will help keep us from living addicted lifestyles so we can live a life of liberty in Jesus Christ. "Jesus said to him, 'You shall love the Lord your God with all your heart, with all your soul, and with all your mind.' This is the first and great commandment and the second is like it: 'You shall love your neighbor as yourself'" (Matthew 22:37-39, NKJV). Our relationship with Abba Father will bring about an external and internal transformation. An external transformation will affect our habits which will change the patterns of our lifestyle. Speech, what we say and how we say it, changes as well. Temperament, the transformation of our personality, will change. Preferences, transformation of what we choose, will change. Internal transformation is a heart transformation. "As in water face reflects face, so man's heart reveals the man" (Proverbs 27:19, NKJV). A change of heart will lead to a change of actions and attitude. The lifestyle of denial is not a consideration with a heart that's willing to change.

We acknowledge the crisis that may exist in us and then pursue freedom that comes from knowing Jesus Christ as Lord and Savior. Even believers who know Christ as Lord and Savior sometimes are tempted to lose heart in God. The Bible reassures us that God wants us more than we can ever imagine. "For I am jealous for you with godly jealousy. For I betrothed you to one husband, that I may present you as a chaste virgin to Christ. But I fear, lest somehow, as the serpent deceived Eve by his craftiness, so your minds may be corrupted from the simplicity that is in Christ" (2 Corinthians 11:2-3, NKJV).

The path to disaffection with God comes when we believe as Eve did that God can't meet all our needs. God is the author of our destiny. Liberty in Christ is found in fulfilling our God-given destiny, knowing the gifts and talents given to us are to be used for the glory of God. No matter how bad our past was, Jesus Christ has changed our lives into lives of freedom from any type of addiction through His grace, which was displayed on the cross of Calvary where Jesus bore our sins. This freedom that comes from Christ needs our cooperation by surrendering the strongholds that consist of wrong beliefs, bad attitudes, unforgiveness, soul ties and layers of self-protection.

When we become new believers in Christ, we are born into a

new family: the family of God. No longer do we have to live under the curse from our natural heritage. No longer do we have to try to figure out who we are or who we can be based upon our genes or psychological makeup or the environment in which we were raised. The only problem we may have as new believers is knowing how to let go of our self-perceived human limitations in order to begin living as new creatures in full fellowship with God. The flawed concepts of God are framed around old mindsets formed from dealing with the authority figures in our lives.

Another is living in the past rather than the truth of God's character found in the Bible. We can be set free in Christ to live productive lives that serve others and bring glory to God through Jesus Christ. The following are Scripture verses that will encourage us.

- "Let your light so shine before men, that they may see your good works and glorify your Father in heaven" (Matthew 5:16, NKJV).
- "Therefore if the Son makes you free, you shall be free indeed" (John 8:36, NKJV).
- "But now having been set free from sin, and having become slaves of God, you have your fruit to holiness, and the end, everlasting life" (Romans 6:22, NKJV).
- "Now the Lord is the Spirit; and where the Spirit of the Lord is, there is liberty" (2 Corinthians 3:17, NKJV).
- "Stand fast therefore in the liberty by which Christ has made us free, and do not be entangled again with the yoke of bondage" (Galatians 5:1, NKJV).

We have liberty in Christ that frees us from the power and the effects of addictions and from an evil mind as stated in 1 Peter 2:16: "As free, yet not using liberty as a cloak for vice, but as bondservants of God" (NKJV). This freedom that comes from Christ heals shattered lives and brings hope to the addicted. The Word of God transforms our minds to wholeness, which changes our behavior and lifestyle into lives that bring glory and honor to the God of the Bible.

Jesus Christ brings true freedom spiritually, which affects our entire lives, and those around us will be affected in a positive way.

A SAVIOR OF LOVE

Love is a Savior
Who bore our great shame,
A man cursed and laughed at,
Mocked and maimed.
He suffered and bled in agony,
But He prayed, "Father, they just don't see."

His heart is heavy
When we walk right on by;
Never a thank-you,
We're too busy to cry.
Father, forgive me, I'm so sorry
For all the hurting I have caused thee.

Jesus is love;
He loves us all.
Sinner and saint, can't you hear His call?
For Jesus is calling,
"Please come unto Me,
For I'm the one who died for thee."

Oh, love is a man
Who heals the lame,
And love is the whisper
Of His dear name.
Oh, love was something
I knew nothing of
Until I met God's gift,
A Savior of love.

By R. J. Thompson

CHAPTER THREE

WINNING THE WAR IN OUR FAMILIES AND RELATIONSHIPS

SELAH SELECTION

"Abide in Me, and I in you. As the branch cannot bear fruit of itself, unless it abides in the vine, neither can you, unless you abide in Me" (John 15:4, NKJV). Depending on Jesus Christ gives us the strength we need for all relationships. The unattached branch does not understand the nature of bearing fruit in life: the fact that he can do nothing—cannot live and produce life—apart from Christ.

CRISIS IN THE HOME

Marriages are under attack. Everyday pressures can lead to a cycle of disaffection and divorce. Unfortunately many marriages today are ending in divorce. The everyday pressures that work against marriages are stress factors such as finances, physical illness and job demands. The Bible tells us of satanic assaults in 1 Peter 5:8: "Be sober, be vigilant; because your adversary the devil walks about like a roaring lion, seeking whom he may devour" (NKJV). The devil is out to destroy marriages; the devil wants to break the covenant of marriage.

The following Scripture verses tell about subjects that can lead to the destruction of marriage.

- "A soft answer turns away wrath, but a harsh word stirs up anger" (Proverbs 15:1, NKJV).
- "A perverse man sows strife, and a whisperer separates the best of friends" (Proverbs 16:28, NKJV).
- "The beginning of strife is like releasing water; therefore stop contention before a quarrel starts" (Proverbs 17:14, NKJV).
- "Make no friendship with an angry man, and with a furious man do not go" (Proverbs 22:24, NKJV).

The Old Testament book of Proverbs tells of the difficulties of living with a contentious, quarrelsome marriage partner. Living in such an environment is like listening to a "constant dripping on a rainy day." It should be remembered that marital conflict often is a symptom of something deeper, such as selfishness, lack of love, unwillingness to forgive, anger, bitterness, communication problems, anxiety, sexual abuse, drunkenness, feelings of inferiority, sin and rebellion, which is a deliberate rejection of God's will for your life. Each of these can cause marital tension.

The Bible speaks to the entire family. First Peter 3:7 says, "Husbands, in the same way be considerate as you live with your wives, and treat them with respect as the weaker partner and as heirs with you of the gracious gift of life, so that nothing will hinder your prayers" (NIV). When we mistreat our wives God won't even listen to our prayers.

Ephesians 6:1-4 says, "Children, obey your parents in the Lord, for this is right. 'Honor your father and mother' which is the first commandment with a promise 'that it may go well with you and that you may enjoy long life on the earth.' Fathers, do not exasperate your children; instead, bring them up in the training and instruction of the Lord" (NIV).

Ephesians 5:22 says, "Wives, submit to your own husbands, as to the Lord" (NKJV).

The Bible shows what happens when discipline is neglected, by the example of Eli and his sons in 1 Samuel 2:12-17. The description of the sons is found in 1 Samuel 2:22-25; the description of what they did is in 1 Samuel 2:27-29; God warns Eli in 1 Samuel 3:11-13; the reason for their demise is found in 1 Samuel 4:11; the demise of the sons and Eli's death are found in 1 Samuel 2:18.

In Ephesians 5:21 Paul speaks both to husbands and wives, saying, "Submit to one another out of reverence for Christ" (NIV). In Philippians 2:3 we read, "Do nothing out of selfish ambition or vain conceit, but in humility consider others better than yourselves" (NIV). And in Ephesians 5:25 Paul reminds us, "Husbands, love your wives, just as Christ loved the church and gave himself up for her" (NIV). Unwillingness to change and insensitivity to each other can often lead to marital tension. There must be the defeat of denial. Many times this tension centers on the issue of physical intimacy or the issue of roles.

With the issue of physical intimacy most couples will experience some kind of problem. These problems may include lack of accurate knowledge, unrealistic expectations which may be the results of pornography and a life of fantasy, fear of not being able to perform adequately, differences in sexual drive, exceptional busyness and/or insensitivity in one or both of the partners. When these problems are not resolved the marriage will suffer, and the home will be in crisis.

Concerning the issue of roles, traditional male-female roles have changed, and this could be a source of tension in the home. The uncertainty of the roles can lead to a spirit of competition and feeling threatened, which can lead to shattered lives and shattered families. The Word of God is still the answer for homes in crisis. The book of James, chapter 4, in the Bible tells us where many crises come from. James asks where wars and fights come from among you. Don't they come from our desires for pleasure that war in our members? Many crises can find their source in selfishness. To overcome crises in the home, preventive actions may be taken, especially by the church, small group Bible studies and/or Sunday school classes. The Holy Bible still has the answer for home crises.

One preventive action is to teach biblical principles of marriage. Christians believe God, who created both male and female and initiated marriage, has also given guidelines for marriage in the pages of Scripture. We live in a society that promotes nonbiblical values about physical intimacy and marriage, so the biblical teaching about love and physical intimacy needs to be reinforced. The importance of marriage, marriage enrichment and marital commitment must be stressed. For most people, life consists of a number of demands, commitments and responsibilities. Often in the midst of these pressures one's marriage and family are slowly shunted to a lesser order of priority. Work, church, community responsibilities and other activities take precedence over time spent with one's spouse. We must find ways to do things together and for each other.

Learning principles of communication and conflict resolution can be an important prevention action. Couples need to learn the importance of listening, mutual acceptance, understanding, empathy, warmth and genuineness toward each other and that these can always be improved. These attributes can be learned expressions in a marriage.

The crisis expressed in the family of Isaac and Rebekah was lived out in their children, Jacob and Esau, as told in Genesis 25:19-34; 27:1-26 (NKJV). The mother and father in this biblical account were distant from each other and were not open with each other. They disagreed about their sons: Rebekah favored Jacob; Isaac favored their firstborn, Esau. Rebekah was closer and more open with Jacob than her own husband, whom she loved. Isaac was closer and more open with Esau. The distance between Isaac and Rebekah led them to a tragic taking up of favoritism with their two sons. A marriage that stays away from crisis takes into consideration both sets of needs for closeness and distance.

The answer concerning the crisis in the home is found in the Word of God for husbands, wives and children. The Word of God heals shattered families, restores them and gives direction in a confused world.

Another great need for husbands and wives is the need to be flexible. Being flexible is having the ability to respond to new influences; it means to bend and still remain strong.

Another need for husbands and wives to avoid crisis in the home is to live a life of humility. Humility is staying broken before God. It's not demanding our own way even when we are right. It's trusting God to work through you as stated in Philippians 4:13: "I can do all things through Christ who strengthens me" (NKJV). This servanthood and sacrificial giving are seen throughout the Bible. "For you were called to freedom, brethren; only do not turn your freedom into an opportunity for the flesh, but through love serve one another" (Galatians 5:18, NKJV). "Yet it shall not be so among you; but whoever desires to become great among you, let him be your servant. And whoever wants to be first among you, let him be your slave" (Matthew 20:26, NKJV). A servant is teachable and builds unity.

As we humble ourselves to each other as husband and wife, we fulfill Psalm 127:1, which says that if the Lord builds our house we won't labor in vain (NKJV). I Peter 5:6 says, "Therefore humble yourselves under the mighty hand of God, that he may exalt you in due time" (NKJV). In Philippians 2:3-8 we read, "Let nothing be done through selfish ambition or conceit, but in lowliness of mind let each esteem others better than himself. Let each of you look out not only for his own interests, but also for the interests of others. Let this mind be in you which was also in Christ Jesus, who, made himself of no reputation, taking the form of a bondservant, and coming in the likeness of men. And being found in appearance as a man, he humbled himself and became obedient to the point of death, even death of the cross" (NKJV). Humbling ourselves before one another can stop a crisis in the home. The Bible teaches us to be willing to sacrifice for one another.

Many lives have been shattered because of selfishness and unwillingness to be flexible. Ecclesiastes 7:8 declares, "The end of a thing is better than it's beginning; the patient in spirit is better than the proud in spirit" (NKJV). Patience, flexibility, humility and sacrificial giving to each other are the ways we can avoid a crisis in our homes. Ephesians 5:21 tells us to submit to one another in the fear of God.

A godly marriage is built on knowing and applying God's Word to our relationship to have a Christ-centered home. First Corinthians 13:4-8 says, "Love suffers long and is kind; love does not envy; love does not parade itself, is not puffed up; does not behave rudely, does not seek its own, is not provoked, thinks no evil; does not rejoice in iniquity, but rejoices in the truth; bears all things, believes all things, endures all things. Love never fails" (NKJV).

TROUBLED RELATIONSHIPS AND ABANDONMENT

The Holy Bible is therapeutic; it has a healing effect on your entire life, helping you to have healthy relationships. Psalm 1:1-3 says, "Blessed is the man who walks not in the counsel of the ungodly, nor stands in the path of sinners,nor sits in the seat of the scornful; but his delight is the law of the Lord, and in his law he meditates day and night. He shall be like a tree planted by the rivers of water, that brings forth its fruit in its season, whose leaf also shall not wither; and whatsoever he does shall prosper" (NKJV).

Shattered lives bring ingrained problems in the lives of people. Many times these people are called "difficult" people, having ingrained patterns of behavior or traits in thinking, behaving, feeling or perceiving that make them more susceptible to relationship problems, conflicts and hot emotions. All relationships can be difficult. Relationships take effort and hard work. Difficult people perceive the world a certain way. They are usually inflexible; these patterns influence their thinking, affections and emotions. Because of these traits they can be depressed or have compulsive disorders. Because they don't recognize their problem, it happens over and over. The Word of God is like a mirror; it shows us who we really are. "But he who looks into the perfect law of liberty and continues in it, and is not a forgetful hearer but a doer of the work, this one will be blessed in what he does" (James 1:25, NKJV). James gives the further admonition: "So speak and so do as those who will be judged by the law of liberty" (2:12, NKJV).

Another reason for these relationship problems is because many carry around internal images, and many times they react to what's happening inside them instead of the subject at hand. Our relationship with our Father in heaven is very important concerning our relationship with others.

"I am the true vine, and my Father is the vinedresser. Every branch in me that does not bear fruit he takes away; and every branch that bears fruit he prunes, that it bear more fruit. You are already clean because of the word which I have spoken to you. Abide in me, and I in you. As the branch cannot bear fruit of itself, unless it abides in the vine, neither can you, unless you abide in me. I am the vine, you are the branches. He who abides in me, and I in him, bears much fruit; for without me you can do nothing. If anyone does not abide in me, he is cast out as a branch and is withered; and they gather them and throw them into the fire, and they are burned. If you abide in me, and my words abide in you, you will ask what you desire, and it shall be done for you. By this my Father is glorified, that you bear much fruit; so you will be my disciples. As the Father loved me, I also have loved you; abide in my love. If you keep my commandments, you will abide in my love, just as I have kept my Father's commandments and abide in his love. These things I have spoken to you, that my joy may remain in you, and that your joy may be full" (John 15:1-11, NKJV).

Jesus Christ showed us the importance of being one with God. "That they all may be one, as you, Father, are in me, and I in you; that they also may be one in us, that the world may believe that you sent me. And the glory which you gave me I have given them, that they may be one just as we are one; I in them, and you in me; that they may be made perfect in one, and that the world may know that you have sent me, and have loved them as you have loved me" (John 17:21-23, NKJV). Our relationship with our heavenly Father is critical for our relationships with all others on earth. The unconditional love of our Father flows to our human relationships.

Troubled people whose lives have been shattered are in bondage to behaviors that cause them not to have healthy relationships. One example is the aggressive controller; these people do not know the meaning of give and take. They never admit being wrong. And the only kind of relationship they are willing to have is with a person who will surrender to their demands. Another example is the indirect manipulators. On the surface these people may seem harmless enough, even nice, but below the surface there is a calculating ability to get their way. They are very good at making people feel guilty when they don't meet their expectations. They are masters at sidestepping the issues and putting the monkey on your back. There are also the emotional leeches; the relationships they tend to find are one way. When we're in relationship with the God of the Bible we give up control because God is in control.

We can communicate with those who seek to be in control, objectively, respectfully and humbly. We need to confront them in love. We need to be constantly redemptive and pursue everyone's highest well-being. The object is not to win the argument but win over a friend. Be willing to see and acknowledge your own mistakes and shortcomings. Remember God is also working in your life to teach you His ways and develop His character in you; we should speak the truth in love.

Romans 12:18-21 talks to us about relationship: "If it is possible, as much as depends on you, live peaceably with all men. Beloved, do not avenge yourselves, but rather give place to wrath; for it is written, 'Vengeance is mine, I will repay, says the Lord.' Therefore 'if your enemy is hungry, feed him; if he is thirsty, give him a drink; for in so doing you will heap coals of fire on his head.' Do not be overcome by evil, but overcome evil with good" (NKJV). Hebrews 10:24- reminds us, "And let us consider one another in order to stir up love and good works" (NKJV). In James 1:19 we read, "So then, my beloved brethren, let every man be swift to hear, slow to speak, slow to wrath" (NKJV). And Ephesians 4:22-24 tells us, "That you put off, concerning your former conduct, the old man which grows corrupt according to the deceitful lusts, and be renewed in the spirit of your mind, and that you put on the new man which was created according to God, in true righteousness and holiness" (NKJV). Troubled relationships are results of shattered lives, but the Word of God and the work of Jesus Christ on the cross of Calvary brought us salvation and wholeness so we can have healthy relationships.

The trauma of loss, divorce, and rejection can bring much pain mentally, emotionally, and even spiritually. This kind of trauma can cause a person to be in relationships, yet not be fully committed because of the pain. They have developed what I call a spirit of abandonment. This trauma has left many people shattered and broken. They can break off relationships at any time. Jesus Christ has come to heal the broken hearted, because of what Christ has done for you on the cross, you can trust again. He will never leave you or forsake you. He loves you unconditionally. Isaiah 53 tells us that He understands our pain and He took that pain on the cross for us. He was despised and rejected. He took our pain, grief and sorrow upon himself. What He did on that cross can heal any shattered life.

Without realizing their own defense mechanism, they will stay in control by having a cold shoulder or walking away. They will diminish the relationship slowly, justifying themselves and ultimately walking away. It will not be until they are completely alone that they will consider and wonder why. Abandon the spirit of abandonment today.

GUILT: THE ENEMY OF LOVE

Shattered lives many times are characterized by a life of guilt. The effects of guilt can be devastating. Guilt can affect you physically, emotionally and spiritually. The God of the Bible can heal a life of guilt. In John 8:1-11 John relates the account of Jesus defending the adulterous woman (NKJV). In this passage we find some very significant thoughts and principles about Christ regarding the presence of guilt which has destroyed many relationships. When guilt motivates us we tend to work toward a clear conscience rather than a right relationship.

How did Jesus handle guilt-ridden people? In the Gospel of Luke, chapter 15, Jesus tells of the prodigal son. The father waited for his son; this is what God the Father is willing to do for us because of His great love. In the Gospel of John, chapter 4, John recounts the story of the woman at the well; everybody condemned her, except Jesus, because of His love for humanity. In the Gospel of Luke, chapter 19,

Zacchaeus took advantage of everybody he could; yet Jesus wanted to go to his home. Because Jesus loved him, Zacchaeus gave his heart to Jesus, and his guilt was healed. In Luke 23 Jesus Christ, the Son of God, on the cross of Calvary prayed for those who crucified him and said, "Father, forgive them, for they do not know what they do" (NKJV).

We are a society that seems skilled in rationalizing and blaming, and it's expressed at times in these words: "I come from a dysfunctional home" or "This is just the way I am." Some people are so good at rationalization that they don't take responsibility for anything they do. The road to healing from a life of guilt is taking responsibility for our actions. Psalm 51:19 records David crying out of his guilt. Guilt destroys our confidence in God. Guilt can make us feel insecure because we're worried that someone may find out what we're really like. "The wicked flee when no one pursues, but the righteous are bold as a lion" (Proverbs 28:1, NKJV). Guilt demolishes our relationships. Unconfessed sin will cause us to respond to people in the wrong way.

Why do people feel guilty? Past experiences and unrealistic expectations. An individual's standards of what is right and wrong, good and bad, usually develop in childhood. As thinking and reasoning abilities develop, children learn the standards of their parents and others. Each child comes to understand the difference between right and wrong, and soon there is an awareness of the punishments or other reactions that come when one disobeys. The best response to unrealistic standards is the adoption of realistic standards. God expects us to go forward to Christian maturity. He disapproves of sin and disobedience, but He sent His Son so we could find forgiveness and life in abundance. Surely He does not want us to stay in self-condemnation and guilt feelings.

Parents teach values. Children learn both from what they hear and from the climate in which teaching occurs. If parents or other teachers are rigid, condemning, demanding and unforgiving, children feel like constant failures. This does much to instill prolonged guilt feelings. Christians must be helped to understand God's high standards of morality, which can only be fulfilled through a relationship with the God of the Bible. When we attempt to obey the law, meet social expectations and do the will of God we are less likely to experience guilt. Jesus never relaxed His standards when He talked with the woman caught in adultery. God's standards are perfect, and He never winks at sin. The woman was not to live in sin any more, and it is hoped her life was changed forever.

We are accepted by God, forgiven unconditionally when we confess our sins and assured we can reach a lifestyle that is pleasing to the Lord—all this stems from the relationship we have with the God of the Bible. Overcoming guilt comes through the forgiving power of Jesus Christ. The following Scripture verses attest to this.

- "But there is forgiveness with you, that you may be feared" (Psalm 130:4, NKJV).
- "In him we have redemption through his blood, the forgiveness of sins, according to the riches of his grace" (Ephesians 1:7, NKJV).
- "Blessed are those whose lawless deeds are forgiven, and whose sins are covered" (Romans 4:7, NKJV).
- "And be kind to one another, tenderhearted, forgiving one another, just as God in Christ forgave you" (Ephesians 4:32, NKJV).
- "I write to you, little children, because your sins are forgiven you for his name's sake" (1 John 2:12, NKJV).
- "If we confess our sins, he is faithful and just to forgive us our sins and to cleanse us from all unrighteousness" (1 John 1:9, NKJV).
- "Bless the Lord, O my soul, and forget not all his benefits, who forgives all your iniquities, who heals all your diseases" (Psalm 103:2-3, NKJV).

EATING DISORDERS: YOU ARE WHAT YOU THINK

Many people are obese in America. Shattered lives fall into many addictions. Compulsive overeating can be a spiritual and psychological problem. Changing the way a person thinks about food through the Word of God and the work of the Holy Spirit can bring deliverance to a shattered life. Food and mood are connected. Statements like "I'm not happy with my body," "I'm miserable and unhappy with my life" and "I eat to feel good" expose the connection between food and mood. Compulsive eaters cover and mask inner feelings by overeating. Some try to eat their way to happiness.

Eating disorders can mean eating too much or not eating enough. This bondage to food deals with controlling your moods. If food can make you feel better, then it should make you stay better. The contentment that fulfills can only come through the God of the Bible.

There are some factors to consider in compulsive overeating. This inner problem is related to the emotions, psychological balance and, most important, spiritual well-being. Another is emotional suppression—stuffing oneself with food, trying to fill up the emptiness inside. Many times people think food will solve the problems of loneliness, tiredness, anger, sadness, guilt, depression and/or comfort. The Bible tells us what to do concerning stress in Matthew 6:33: "But seek first the kingdom of God and his righteousness, and all these things shall be added to you" (NKJV). Look what the Bible says in 1 Corinthians 6:12: "All things are lawful for me, but all things are not helpful. All things are lawful for me, but I will not be brought under the power of any" (NKJV). The Bible is telling us through the apostle Paul's life not to be mastered by anything. The biblical process will break us free from the misuse of food.

We know food can't bring ultimate fulfillment to our lives. Faith in Jesus Christ as Lord and Savior; the use of the Bible as the road map to life; the love letter God the Father has written to us, all heal us from a shattered life, and bring balance to our lives as we overcome through the Word of God. Overcomers learn self-discipline. Philippians 3:20 says, "For our conversation (lifestyle) is in heaven; from whence also we look for the Savior, the Lord Jesus Christ" (KJV).

There needs to be a surrender through transformation, as stated in Romans 12:2: "And do not be conformed to this world, but be transformed by the renewing of your mind, that you may prove what is that good and acceptable and perfect will of God" (NKJV). In Romans 12:1 we see freedom through sacrifice: "I beseech you therefore, brethren, by the mercies of God, that you present your bodies as a living sacrifice, holy, acceptable to God, which is your reasonable service" (NKJV).

We are serving God, not ourselves. Our focus needs to be toward God: "Therefore, whether you eat or drink, whatever you do, do all to the glory of God" (1 Corinthians 10:31, NKJV). First Thessalonians 2:12 reminds us, "That ye would walk worthy of God, who hath called you unto his kingdom and glory" (KJV).

MONEY IS A HEART ISSUE

Many relationships have been devastated because of misunderstanding and misappropriation of financial resources, leaving lives shattered and broken. Many people spend their waking hours thinking about money. The preoccupation with money can create an undue amount of stress, anxiety or even anger. Many divorced couples say that financial difficulties were the primary cause of their separation.

The Bible has a lot to say about money management. In the New Testament money is talked about more than heaven and hell combined. Matthew 6:21 states "For where your treasure is, there your heart will be also" (NKJV). Some symptoms of financial bondage include overdue bills, greed, family needs not being met, over commitment to work and covetousness. The lack of control because of an unfulfilled life can only be satisfied by having a relationship with the God of the Bible. The Bible teaches a lot about stewardship. In Matthew 25:14-30 we read the story of a man traveling to a far country, revealing the importance of stewardship (NKJV). The Bible declares God's ownership of everything in Psalm 24:1: "The earth is the LORD'S, and the fullness thereof; the world, and they that dwell therein" (KJV). And in 1 Corinthians 4:1-2 we read, "Let a man so consider us, as servants of Christ and stewards of the mysteries of God. Moreover it is required in stewards that one be found faithful" (NKJV).

Many people are being shattered through gambling. As gambling increases, more and more people are being confronted with the negative impact of gambling in their own lives and the lives of those around them. Compulsive or pathological gambling is a progressive behavior in which an individual has a psychologically uncontrollable preoccupation with an urge to gamble that compromises family, occupation and other pursuits. Any addiction robs us of the important relationships in our lives.

Why do people gamble? For the thrill, the glamour, the lights and the excitement. Many gamble for the money. This is a way to get rich, and yet it's the poor that are funding it. Some gamble for recognition; it makes them feel good and important. Some gamble for control; they feel that they have control over the gambling and have mastered something. Some gamble for connection; they are doing it for relationships—they know the dealers and those around them—and yet their other relationships, such as family members, suffer.

Alcohol is prevalent while gambling. The more you drink, the more likely you are to spend, because of the dullness of your senses. Gambling can lead to other addictions such as stealing and drugs. It can also lead to negative sexual behaviors in order to feel good about yourself after feeling like a failure in gambling.

To break this bondage Psalm 46:1 tells us, "God is our refuge and strength, a very present help in trouble" (NKJV). Someone bigger than us can help us: the God of the Bible. To break this bondage you must realize your need and stop the denial. Compulsive gamblers need help from others and need accountability. They need to admit their need for God to help them overcome their compulsive gambling and realize restoration is possible. "'Now, therefore,' says the LORD, 'Turn to Me with all your heart, with fasting, with weeping, and with mourning.' So rend your heart, and not your garments; return to the LORD your God, for He is gracious and merciful, slow to anger, and great in kindness; And He relents from doing harm" (Joel 2:12-13, NKJV

Submitting yourself in prayer can break this bondage. Psalm 51:17 tells us, "The sacrifices of God are a broken spirit, a broken and a contrite heart- these, O God, you will not despise" (NKJV). You must realize that you must not return to gambling. Psalm 26:11 declares, "But as for me, I will walk in my integrity; redeem me and be merciful to me" (NKJV).

Your life is a gift from God. You have a destiny to fulfill that only you can fulfill. Others need you: your family, friends and those you are yet to meet. This unconditional love that comes from the God of the Bible can break any bondage by your receiving Jesus Christ as Lord and Savior. The chains that bind you can be broken, and a new life can begin through the power or unconditional love that comes from the God of the Bible.

POEM PAUSE

IT IS HIS LOVE

It's not the messenger, but the message;
It's not the music, but the words;
It's not the beauty of the voices
But that the gospel's heard.
For the only thing that matters
Is that your heart truly believes.
Reach out for He is calling;
His love you can receive

It is His love;
It was the cross,
God's Son who died.
But all's not lost.
He rose again;
He lives to tell
Jesus our Lord
Defeated hell.

It's not by works that we are given
This priceless gift of love.
But by faith we can receive it,
This gift from God above.
More precious than fine silver,
It's worth far more than gold.
There is no price tag on it;
It can't be bought or sold.

It is His love;
It was the cross,
God's Son who died.
But all's not lost.
He rose again;
He lives to tell
Jesus our Lord
Defeated hell.

By R. J. Thompson

CHAPTER FOUR

NEW LIFE IN CHRIST

SELAH SELECTION

"If then you were raised with Christ, seek those things which are above, where Christ is, sitting at the right hand of God. And have put on the new man who is renewed in knowledge according to the image of Him who created him" (Colossians 3:1, 10, NKJV).

The transformation that comes from repenting of sin and accepting Jesus Christ as Lord and Savior gives a new life spiritually. Believers have clothed themselves with a brand-new nature that is continually being renewed. The "new nature" from Christ frees us from sin, sets our hearts on "things above" (3:1) and gives us the hope of eternity. The new man is one's new, regenerated humanity—including a new spirit, a new nature and a new life.

NEW BEGINNINGS THROUGH CHRIST JESUS

Shattered lives believe there is no hope for them, but in Christ Jesus we find life and hope for a new beginning. In society you can see this through New Year's resolutions; people are looking for ways to start over. "Therefore, if anyone is in Christ, he is a new creation; old things have passed away; behold, all things have become new" (2 Corinthians 5:17, NKJV). Galatians 6:15 reminds us, "For in Christ Jesus neither circumcision nor uncircumcision avails anything, but a new creation" (NKJV). When we receive Christ as Savior and Lord and repent of our sins, we become a new creature in Jesus Christ.

Our Father in heaven shows us the real meaning of love. In 1 Corinthians 13:1-13 we read of unconditional love, how God loves us and what He put inside us. This kind of love suffers long, and is kind, does not envy, does not parade itself, is not puffed up, does not behave rudely, does not seek its own, is not easily provoked, thinks no evil, does not rejoice in iniquity, but rejoices in the truth. Bears all things, believes all things, hopes all things, and endures all things. Love never fails (NKJV).

This new life teaches us in Ephesians 4:15, "Speaking the truth in love, may grow up in all things into Him who is the head- Christ" (NKJV). This new beginning and new life in Christ bring us hope because we see a better future. This new beginning affects our bodies; our bodies are a channel of God's love. This new life also affects our thought life: "Finally, brethren, whatever things are true, whatever things are noble, whatever things are just, whatever things are pure, whatever things are lovely, whatever things are of good report, if there is any virtue and if there is anything praiseworthy-meditate on these things" (Philippians 4:8, NKJV).

This new life also affects our feelings. Philippians 4 teaches us to rejoice in the Lord, which helps our feelings. Our behavior changes, and the bondages are broken by the application of the Word of God. This new life is expressed spiritually and is the ultimate goal for our spiritual life, for "if we live in the Spirit, let us also walk in the Spirit" (Galatians 5:25, NKJV). Our spiritual life shows others we are living a disciplined life. Our new life in Christ gives us a new identity. The world's standards and views no longer manipulate us concerning who we are or what we do. "This I say, therefore, and testify in the Lord, that you should no longer walk as the rest of the Gentiles walk, in the futility of their mind, having their understanding darkened, being alienated from the life of God, because of the ignorance that is in them, because of the blindness of their heart; who, being past feelings, having given themselves over to lewdness, to work all uncleanness with greediness. But you have not so learned Christ" (Ephesians 4:17-20 NKJV).

Shattered lives can find hope in the person of Jesus Christ, who transforms lives and gives hope for the future. He came to heal broken, addictive, compulsive, out-of-balance lives. He came to give life and give it more abundantly, as stated in John 10:10 (NKJV).

WHOLENESS THROUGH CHRIST JESUS

Isaiah 61:1 reveals that Jesus came to the brokenhearted. He came to restore shattered lives. Wholeness has to do with inward peace, about who you are, what you're doing and where you're going—individually and with the relationships around you. When you know God's purpose for your life, you won't leave this life with an unfulfilled destiny that could have helped others. The way to wholeness is to release the past, confess when you have sinned and release others who have sinned against you. God's Word is God's love letter to us and our road map in this life. In obeying God's Word we are brought to wholeness, walking in deliverance by keeping far from those things that separate us from God. As we press toward the mark, we will use failure as a stepping stone to grow, to trust the Lord. Wholeness will involve changing the way we think, feel or act.

Psalm 34:18 reminds us, "The LORD is near to those who have a broken heart, and saves such as have a contrite spirit" (NKJV). We must acknowledge when we are broken, that we can't fix ourselves, and accept God's grace for our lives, provided by Jesus Christ. Jeremiah 18:1-6 describes how God takes the marred piece of pottery and makes it over again (NKJV). Something new has happened; this is what God does to the broken who come to Him in Jesus' name. He makes them whole and new again. All things become new. Jesus still heals shattered lives and brings wholeness to the brokenhearted.

We live in a world filled with broken people and broken relationships. The Word of God still has the answer for the brokenness of this world. "I have been crucified with Christ; it is no longer I who live, but Christ lives in me; and the life which I now live in the flesh I live by faith in the Son of God, who loved me and gave himself for me" (Galatians 2:20, NKJV). Through Jesus Christ we can live a balanced life, walking in deliverance from addiction, fears, hopelessness, compulsive behavior, depression and anything else that would control our lives other than Jesus Christ, the Son of God. You can take your shattered life to Jesus Christ and trust Him with the pieces; He will put you back together. "For God so loved the world that he gave his only begotten Son, that whoever believes in him should not perish but have everlasting life" (John 3:16, NKJV).

Jesus Christ has come to heal shattered lives, to restore the inner being, to heal our will, our heart and our understanding. The results will be a balanced life of thinking, emotions, passions—all of which affect our appetites. The God of the Bible, through the sacrifice of His Son Jesus Christ, who died for the sins of the world on the cross of Calvary, has the power to restore shattered lives.

CPSIA information can be obtained at www.ICGtesting.com
Printed in the USA
BVOW041410291112

306766BV00001B/68/P